Teach Me About Allah

Khalil Ismail and Umm Zakiyyah

99 Names Series

بِسْمِ ٱللَّهِ ٱلرَّحْمَٰنِ ٱلرَّحِيمِ
قُلْ هُوَ ٱللَّهُ أَحَدٌ ۝١ ٱللَّهُ ٱلصَّمَدُ ۝٢ لَمْ يَلِدْ وَلَمْ يُولَدْ ۝٣ وَلَمْ يَكُن لَّهُۥ كُفُوًا أَحَدٌۢ ۝٤

اللّٰه

What does this mean?

The Qur'an says,

'He is Allah, the One and Only. Allah, the Eternal, the Absolute. He begets not, nor is He begotten And there is none like unto Him.'

Al-Baa'ith, The Resurrector
Ash-Shaheed, The Witness

Ya Allah, when I'm risen from the ground, make me of those who earned your forgiveness

What does this mean?

The Resurrector:

We will all die and go into the ground, but Allah will bring us back to life for the Day of Judgment.

The Witness:

Allah sees everything, even when people don't tell the truth.
And He always knows what really happened.

Yaa Allah, when I'm risen from the ground, make me of those who earned your forgiveness:
O Allah! When you bring me back to life after I die, forgive me for the bad I did, and let me go to Paradise.

Al-Haqq, The Truth, The Real
Al-Wakeel, Disposer of Affairs
I kneel to you

What does this mean?

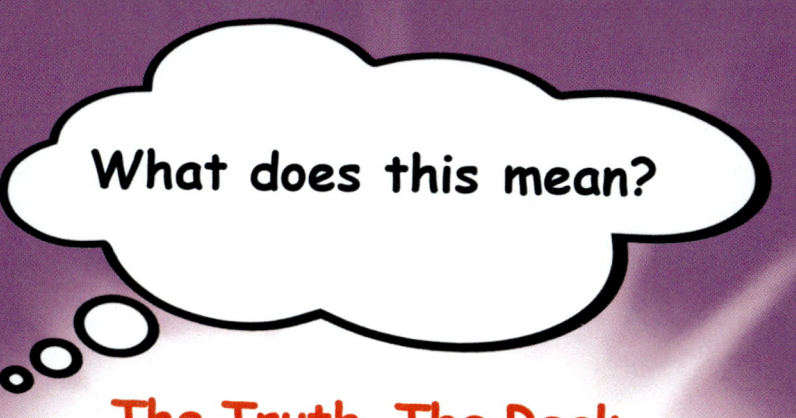

The Truth, The Real:

There is no doubt about the reality of Allah.

Disposer of Affairs:

No matter what happens, Allah can take care of everything and solve every problem.

I kneel to You:
I put my knees on the ground in prayer.

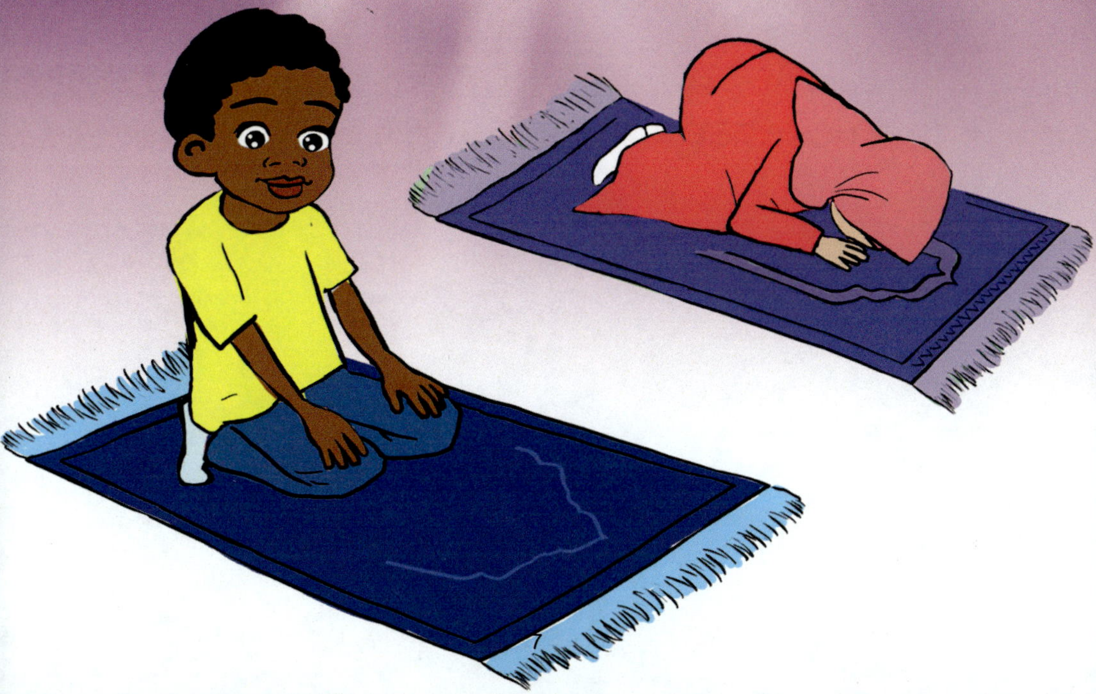

القويّ
المتين

Al-Qawwee, <u>The Most Strong</u>
Al-Mateen, <u>The Firm One</u>
Presence never murky

Al-Muhsee, The Accounter

Al-Mubdih, The Originator

Yaa Allah, make my sins go downward.

What does this mean?

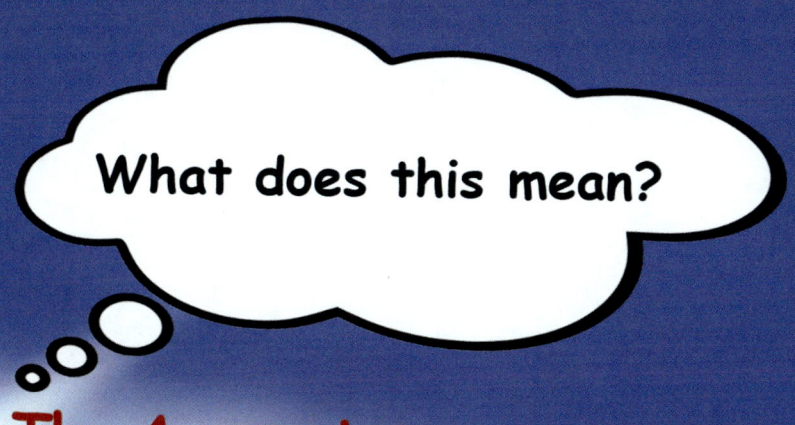

The Accounter:

Allah keeps a record of everything.

The Originator:

Allah created everything when there was nothing.

Yaa Allah, make my sins go downward: O Allah! Take my sins away from me.

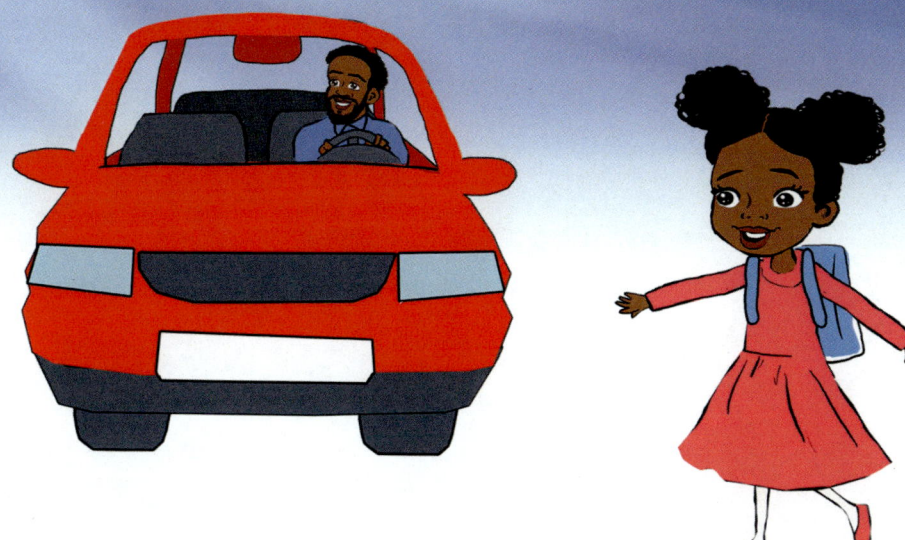

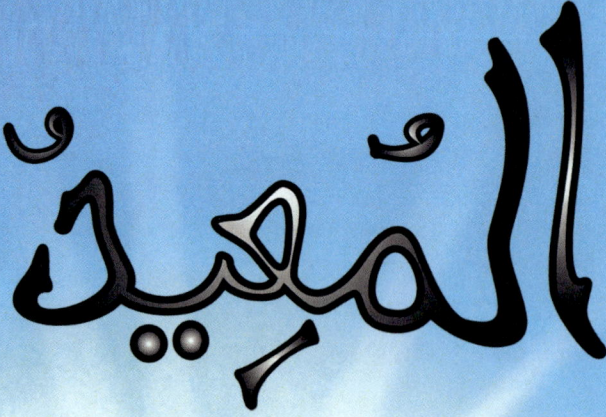

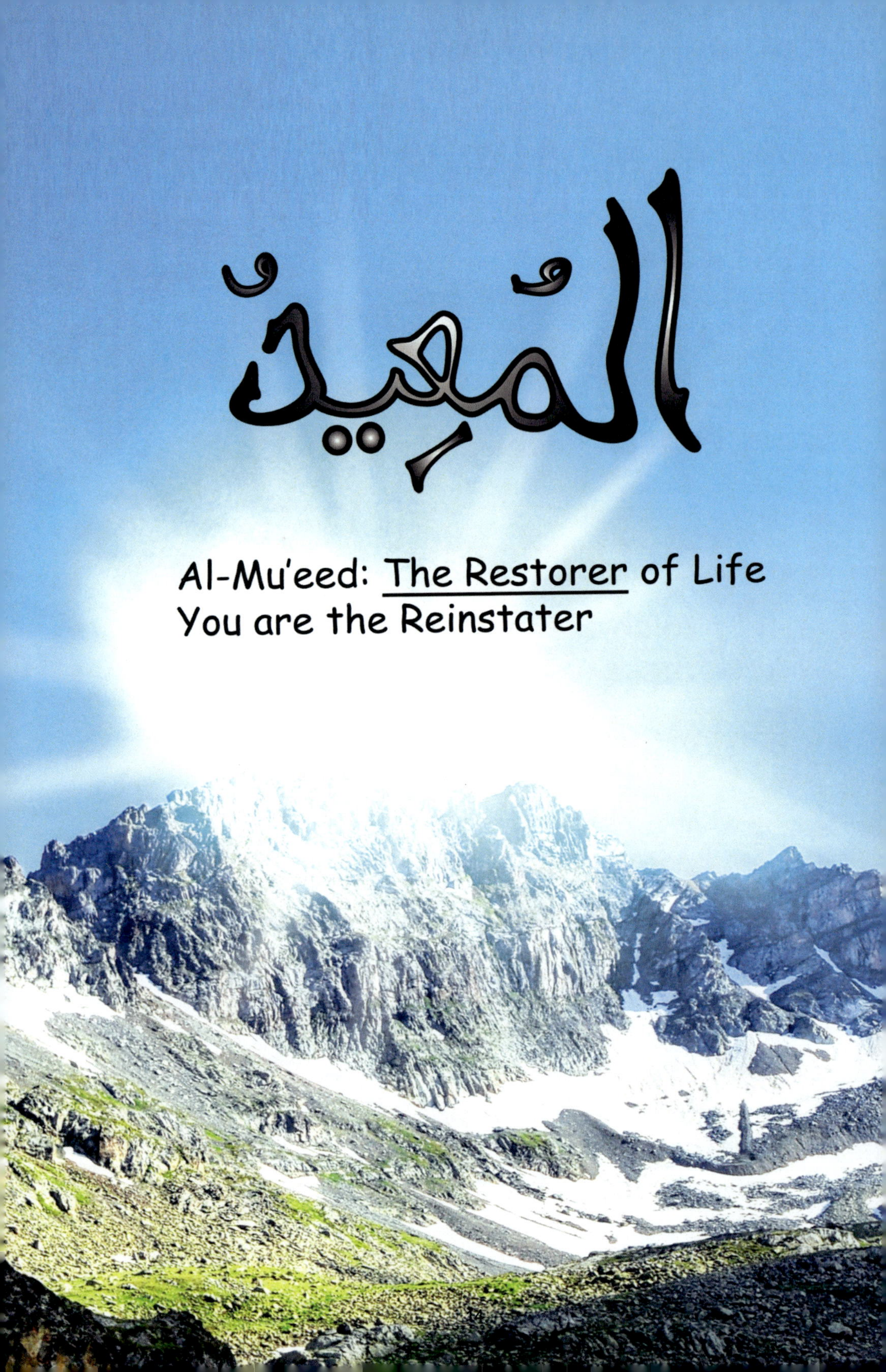
المُعِيدُ
Al-Mu'eed: The Restorer of Life
You are the Reinstater

What does this mean?

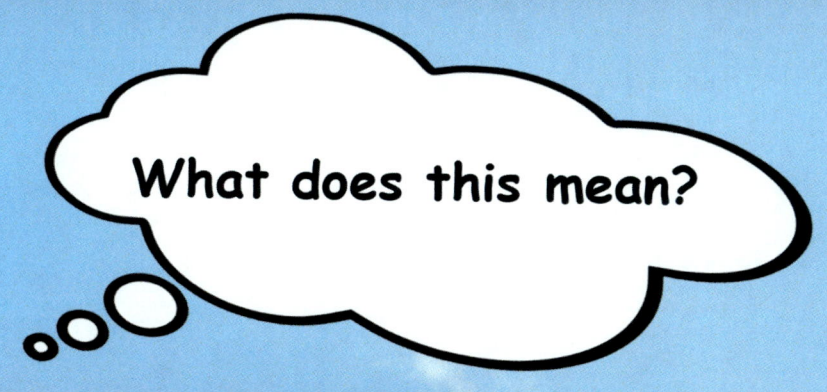

The Restorer of Life:

After we die, Allah will give us life again.

You are the Reinstater:
O Allah! If something is taken away from us, You have the power to give it back.

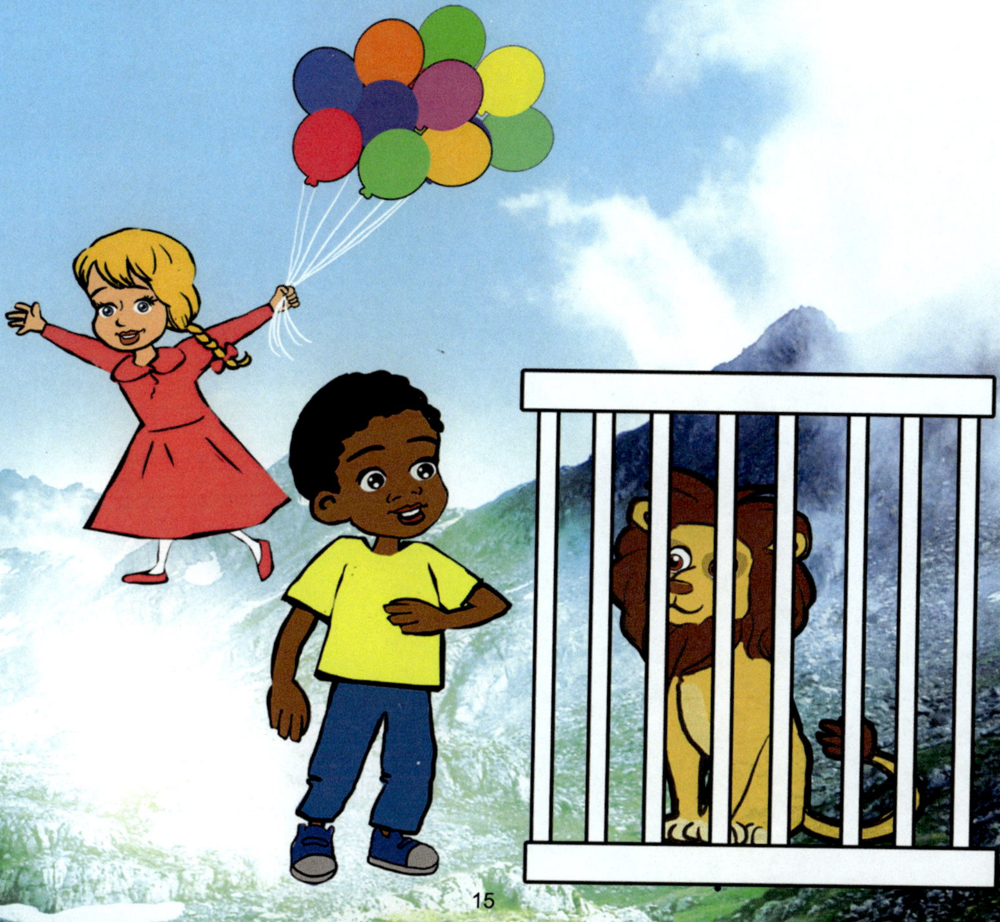

Al-Muhyeey, The Giver of Life

Al-Mumeet, The Causer of Death

> What does this mean?

The Giver of Life:
Allah is the One who created your soul and had it put it in your body.

The Causer of Death:
Allah is the One who tells the angel when to take out your soul.

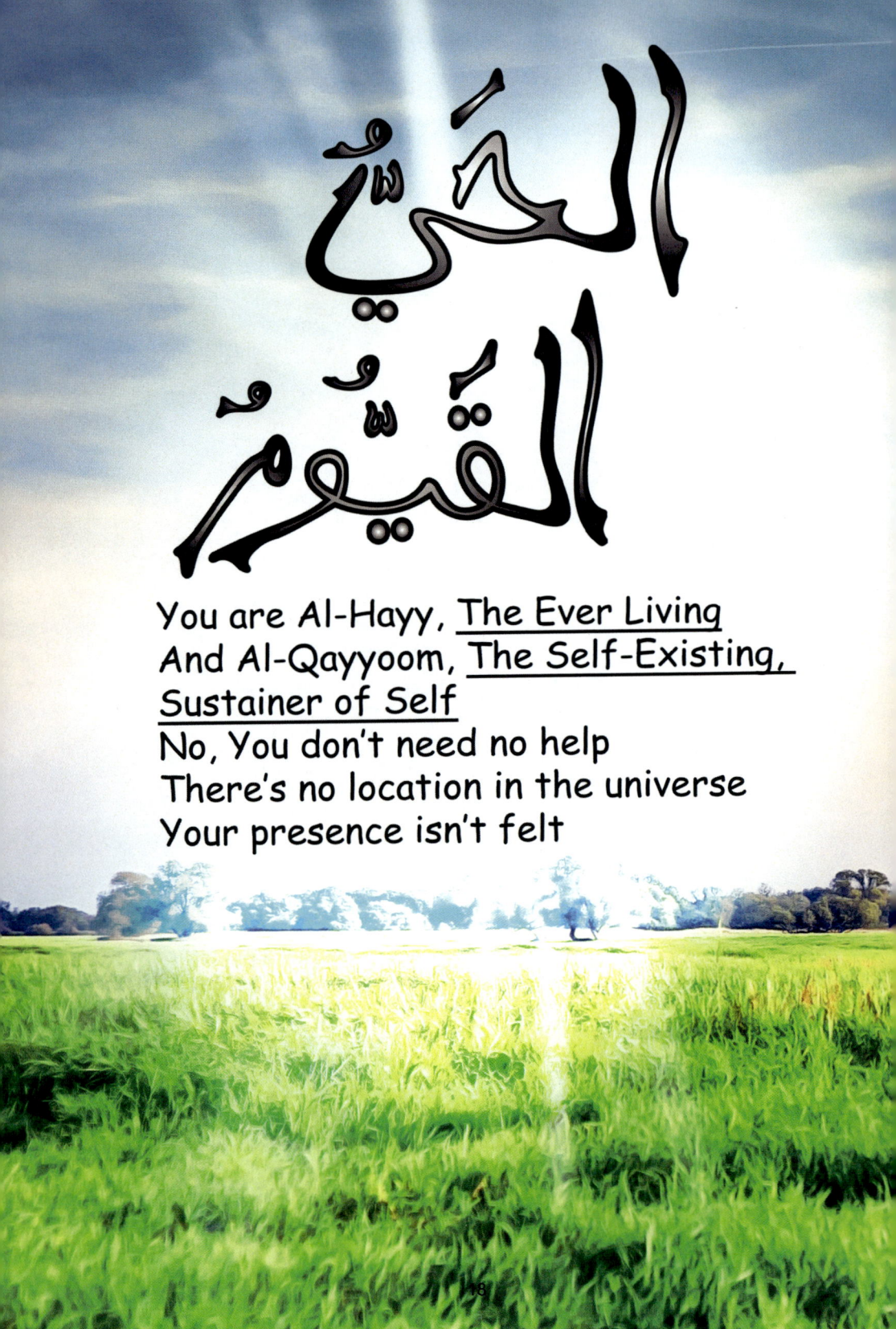

الحَيُّ
القَيُّومُ

You are Al-Hayy, The Ever Living
And Al-Qayyoom, The Self-Existing,
Sustainer of Self
No, You don't need no help
There's no location in the universe
Your presence isn't felt

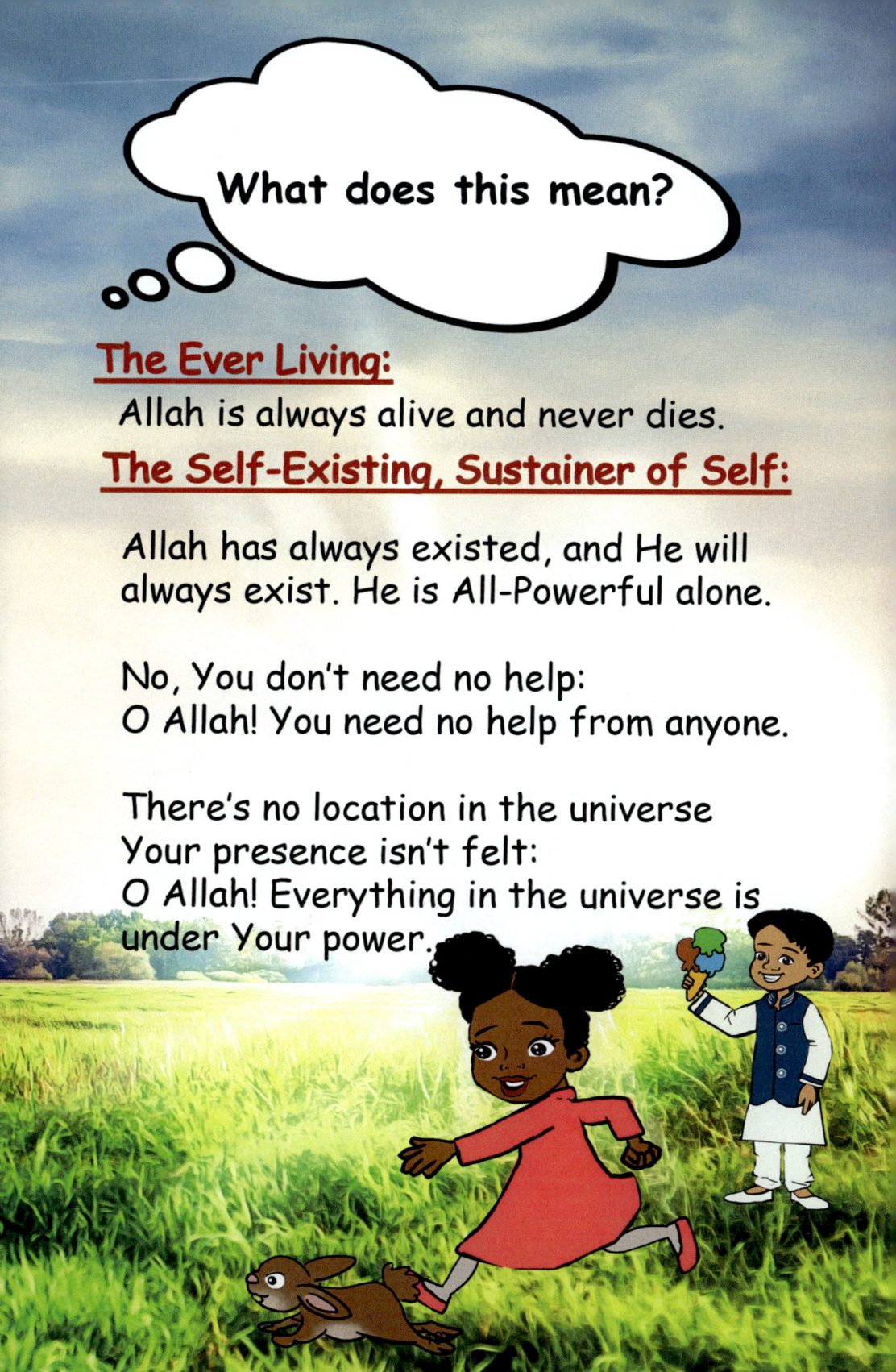

What does this mean?

The Ever Living:
Allah is always alive and never dies.

The Self-Existing, Sustainer of Self:

Allah has always existed, and He will always exist. He is All-Powerful alone.

No, You don't need no help:
O Allah! You need no help from anyone.

There's no location in the universe
Your presence isn't felt:
O Allah! Everything in the universe is under Your power.

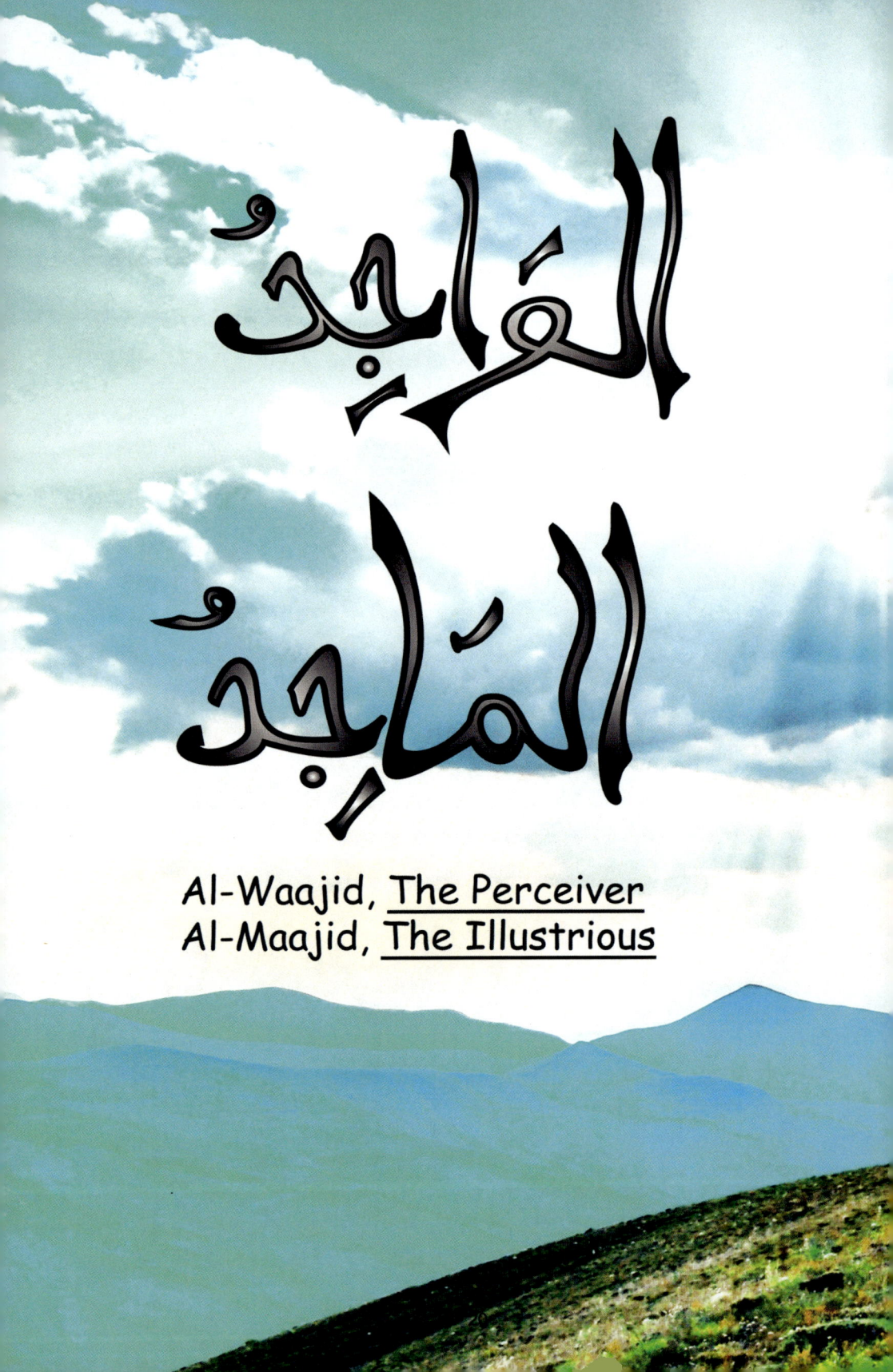

الواجد
الماجد

Al-Waajid, The Perceiver
Al-Maajid, The Illustrious

What does this mean?

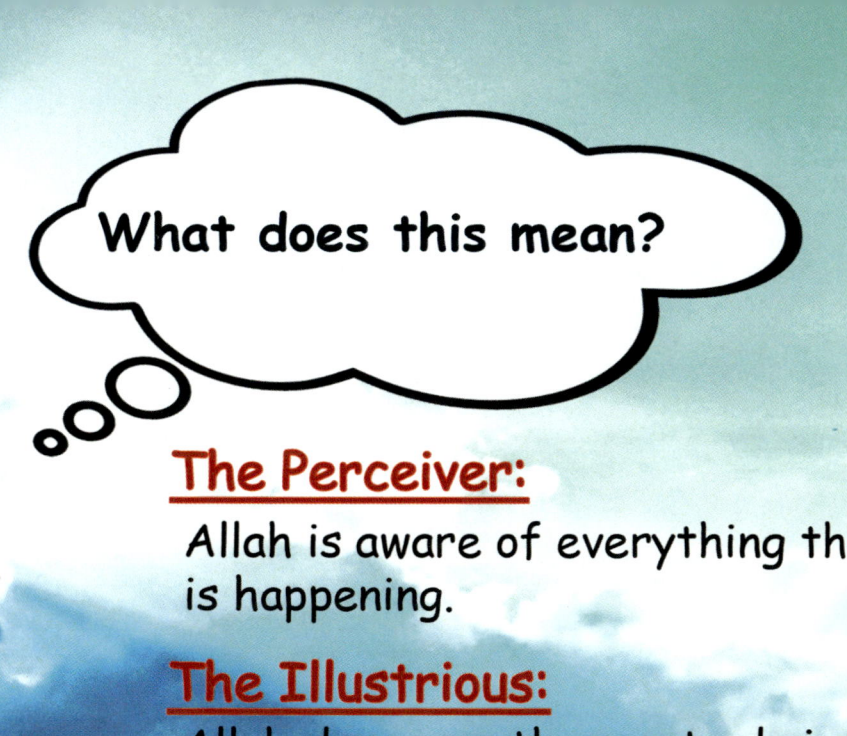

The Perceiver:

Allah is aware of everything that is happening.

The Illustrious:

Allah deserves the most admiration and respect.

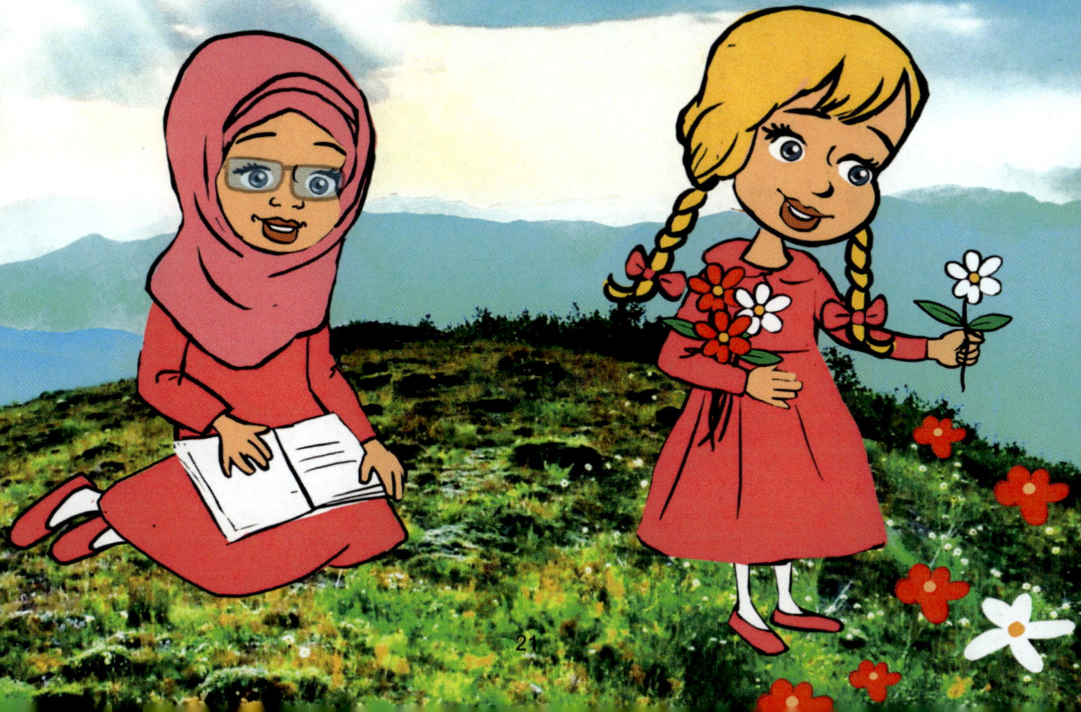

Al-Waahid, <u>The One</u>, The Unique
Yaa Allah, grant us all tawfeeq
Al-Ahad, <u>The One</u>

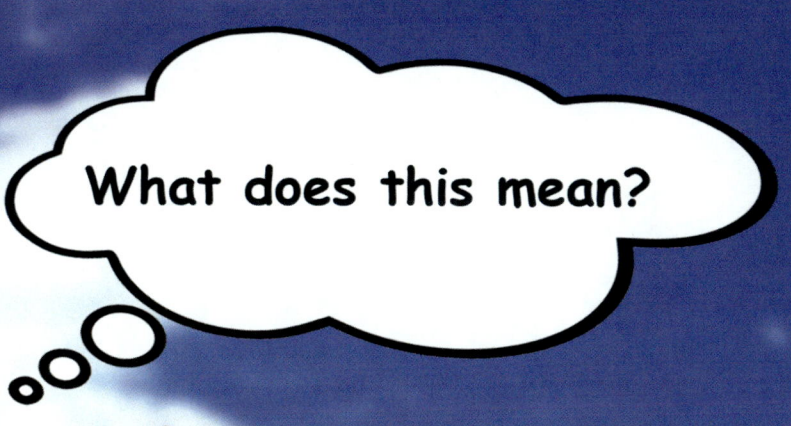

Al-Waahid, The One:

There is nothing and no one like Allah.

Yaa Allah, grant us all tawfeeq:
O Allah!
Give us the ability to remain Muslim until the Day of Judgment.

Al-Ahad, The One:

There is only one God: Allah.

As-Samad, <u>The Eternal</u>
Al-Qaadir, <u>The Omnipotent</u>

Allahu Akbar, Your power so unlimited

The Eternal:

Allah is always independent, and He needs no one.

The Omnipotent:

There is no limit or end to the power of Allah.

Allahu Akbar: Allah is greater than anything and anyone.
Your power so unlimited: O Allah! You are able to do whatever You wish, whenever You wish.

Al-Muqtadir, The Determiner
Al-Muqqaddim, The Expediter

Determiner:
Allah decides what will happen now and in the future.

Expediter:
Allah makes things happen quickly whenever He decides to.

Yaa Allah, You are Al-Mu'akhir,
<u>The Delayer</u>
We must wait until You've decided

The Delayer:

Allah can make things happen later than we want or expect.

We must wait until You've decided: O Allah! Help us be patient as we wait for Your decree.

1. Answer: When you pray, you can say the name Ash-Shaheed.
2. Answer: Al-Walee.
3. Answer: Al-Waajid.

(Quiz: Do simple multiple choice with three options):

1. Someone said I did something that I didn't do, and I know Allah knows what really happened. I want to pray that they find out what really happened. What name should I use?
a. Al-Jabbar
b. Al- Aziz
c. As-Shaheed

2. I want Allah to always help me and protect me. I want Him to be my Friend.
a. Al-Wasi'
b. Al- Mughni
c. As-Walee

3. I lost something and can't find it, but I know Allah is aware of everything and every place. So He knows where it is, and I want Him to help me find it.
a. Al-Waajid
b. Al- Raheem
c. Al-Mumin

Learn the "99 Names" Song

This four-book series is based on the song **"99 Names" by Khalil Ismail**. Listen and download the song at **khalilismail.com** or via any major streaming platform such as Spotify, Apple Music, or YouTube.

Questions? Contact us at **khalilismail.com/contact**

99 Names Series whoisAllah99.com

Made in the USA
Middletown, DE
28 August 2023

37021227R00020